MY TEEN STRUGGLES WITH SAME-SEX ATTRACTIONS

Ben Marshall

Consulting Editor: Dr. Paul Tautges

Help! My Teen struggles With Same-Sex Attractions

© 2011 Ben Marshall

ISBN
Paper: 978-1-63342-030-4
ePub: ISBN 978-1-63342-031-1
Kindle: ISBN 978-1-63342-032-8

Published by Shepherd Press
P.O. Box 24
Wapwallopen, PA 18660

www.shepherdpress.com

All Scripture quotations, unless stated otherwise,
are from the New American Standard Bible
(The Lockman Foundation, 1995).

First printed by Day One Publications

Designed by **documen**

Contents

INTRODUCTION

The only time Jon could remember feeling like this was when he learned that his younger brother had died in a tragic bike accident. Memories flooded his mind, making him realize that the future was going to be very different from now on. He felt anger at not being able to do anything to change the situation; anger at wishing he had stepped in to prevent this from happening when he saw the early signs. All this and more swept through his mind, creating the feeling that he was under water, watching the surface slip further and further away.

Jon's conversation with his son Matt had started so innocently. He remembered that Matt had approached him earlier in the week and, with a sheepish look on his face, had asked Jon if he could talk to him about something. Jon thought for sure it was about dating, girls, and everything else that went along with Matt's season of life. Matt was thirteen years old and going through puberty. Jon decided that he was going to take Matt out for a burger and fries so they could be alone and have the talk that Jon had dreamed about. He could not have imagined a better scenario as he unwrapped his burger and watched Matt dip his fries into the ketchup.

It wasn't until Matt had talked at length about his health class at school and the biology of sex, the lesson in Sunday-school class about Billy who had two dads, and the sleepover he had had at Doug's house, that reality came crashing in. Jon heard very little after the phrase, "Dad, I think I'm gay." Jon tried to grasp what was going on, but it was too much to handle. He had no idea what to do or where to turn.

Can you identify with Jon? If you can, believe me, you are not alone. This mini-book is designed to be a guide for any Christian parent whose son or daughter reveals that he or she is struggling with same-sex attractions. I hope that it will answer some of your questions about what to do in a situation such as this. However, more than simply find answers to questions, it is my earnest desire that you will receive real hope that leads to real change.

1

The Magnitude of the Problem: What We're up Against

Try as we might, it is almost impossible to escape from the impact that homosexuality has had on life in the twenty-first century. "Gay marriage", "life partner", "alternative lifestyle", "gay pride"—these phrases are all commonplace in today's culture. The subject of homosexuality is perhaps one of the most hotly debated today, both in the secular world and within Christian circles.

The world has offered many different explanations for homosexuality, all sounding as though they have good scientific proof. At the forefront of this debate is the argument that people are born or created with a tendency to be attracted to the same sex instead of to the opposite sex. This can lead to a great deal of frustration for the parent of a teenager who claims that he or she is struggling with homosexual thoughts and desires. If the world's explanation is true, there is no need to dig into the Scriptures to see what

God has to say about this topic. However, if that explanation is false, and man is not created with homosexual tendencies, there is great reason to search through the Scriptures, not only to see what is said about this issue, but also to find out how to help those who are toying with this sin as well as those who have already fallen prey to its temptations.

Homosexuality has traditionally been viewed by Christians as an abomination in the sight of God. This understanding goes back to the first chapters of Scripture, from the account of God's wrath poured upon the cities of Sodom and Gomorrah as judgment for their sin (Genesis 18–19). Today, however, those in a church who fall into this sin are usually treated in one of two ways: either the church excommunicates the one caught up in the sin without going through the proper steps of discipline described in Matthew 18:15–21, or the sin is overlooked and hidden so that the mainstream congregation is kept away from it. Thus the sin of homosexuality is usually not spoken of or handled biblically, and parents are left in the dark as to what to do if their child expresses to them that he or she is dealing with homosexual thoughts and desires. God's Word does not exhort the church to excommunicate the homosexual sinner immediately or call for the sin to be hidden; but neither does it condone homosexual behavior. Romans 1:18–32 clearly states that homosexuality is the result of mankind exchanging the worship of God the Creator for the worship of the creation.

Through many different avenues, the sin of homosexuality has not only become ordinary and normal, it has also become a widely accepted practice in the world today. For parents like Jon in the Introduction, the amount of scientific and psychological "evidence" that is available through the Web, textbooks, TV shows, and a whole host of other media seems overwhelmingly to paint the picture that people cannot help whether or not they are homosexual.[1] This push for acceptance is perhaps most obvious through our culture's attempt to make homosexuality an issue of biology.

Attempt to Explain Homosexuality through Biology

While history indicates that homosexuality has been a major part of different societies, the sexual revolution that paved the road for today's homosexual movement can be traced back to a sex researcher in 1948. That researcher, Alfred Kinsey, studied sexual behavior in males by interviewing 5,300 men. Of these, 10 percent claimed to have been homosexual for at least three years.[2] From that point forward, scientists with a heavy evolutionary bent have spent large amounts of time and money attempting to prove that homosexuality is biological in nature and cannot be helped.

In 1991, Simon LeVay of the West Hollywood Institute for Gay and Lesbian Education in Los Angeles conducted a study aimed at proving that homosexuality is biological in origin. This study dealt specifically with the differences between the hypothalamus in homosexual men versus that in heterosexual men.[3] While many cite this study as proof that homosexuality is indeed biological in nature, LeVay himself is quoted as saying, "It's important to stress what I didn't find. I did not prove that homosexuality is genetic, or find a genetic cause for being gay. I didn't show that gay men are born that way, the most common mistake people make in interpreting my work."[4] In the same year, Drs. Bailey and Pillard sought to prove through genetic reasoning that homosexuality had biological roots. Dr. Bailey's report, however, showed that no such conclusion could be drawn.[5]In 1993, another study dealing with genes and homosexuality was conducted by

Dean Hamer. In order to prove the existence of a gay gene, he looked at two brothers who were practising homosexuals. At best, this study could conclude only that the brothers were related.

As recently as 2005, further studies were conducted in an attempt to prove that the homosexual male's brain responds more in line with a woman's brain than with that of a heterosexual male. Researchers at the Karolinska Institute in Stockholm, Sweden, published an article on May 10, 2005 in the journal *Proceedings of the National Academy of Sciences* stating that the male homosexual's brain responded like the brain of a woman when he sniffed a chemical from the male hormone testosterone.[6] The only outcome of this study was the conclusion that homosexual men seem to be attracted to the smells of men much like women are physically attracted to the smells of men. This merely reveals a connection between the things that women and homosexual men prefer to smell. These preferences could change with time and are not necessarily linked biologically. For instance, a person might enjoy the smell of hamburgers for a certain period of time. If, however, he or she were to become violently ill from hamburgers, that preference of smell might change.

Implications of Biological Explanations

The biological explanations seek to give the person with same-sex attractions viable reasons for why he or she is different from the heterosexual in sexual orientation. They seek to make the primary cause of homosexuality something that an individual is born with, thus releasing him or her from personal responsibility for such same-sex attraction. However, they do not explain why someone would choose to be homosexual, and they give virtually no hope for any change. Rather, the teenager who is struggling with homosexual thoughts and desires is given the hopeless answer that this is the way that he or she was created. If sexual preference is indeed predetermined at conception by the genes that are given to a person, then that person cannot possibly be at fault for any of the feelings and/or actions that he or she has or commits throughout his or her life. The logical conclusion from this implication is that such people must simply accept themselves for who they are, because they cannot change.

Additionally, the biological explanation attacks the very character of God. If the hypothesis is true, it means that a homosexual was created by God as such, making God the creator of homosexuality.

This would make God extremely unfair and unjust when he then condemns the very thing that he has created a person to be. In addition, God would also be the creator of sin. James 1:13 clearly states that God does not tempt people to sin:

> Let no one say when he is tempted, "I am being tempted by God"; for God cannot be tempted by evil, and He Himself does not tempt anyone.

The conclusions that are reached in a biological explanation do not fit with Scripture. Thus they should not be considered viable reasons to allow homosexual thoughts, desires, or behaviors. While the biological explanation is not valid, it is appropriate to acknowledge that we do live in broken bodies due to the curse of sin. Due to this brokenness, someone may have the propensity to be attracted to the same sex. In cases where this may be true, the individual still has the responsibility and capability to resist those temptations and live the life that God has called him or her to live.

To say the least, it has become increasingly difficult for parents to raise their children in the fear of the Lord without being bombarded with pseudofacts from the scientific and psychological communities. However, the pressure to accept homosexuality comes not only from outside the church, but from inside religious communities as well.

2

Religious Modifications: Changing the Meaning of Scripture

In addition to those trying to prove that homosexuality is biological in nature, some pastors claim that God has created people with tendencies toward the same gender and that the historical church has been sinful in condemning the acts of homosexuality.[7] In the past, the church was seen as a refuge from the philosophies and temptations of the world. However, as society has embraced the sin of homosexuality more and more, many churches have ceased to become a refuge and instead have become an approving voice for the homosexual movement.

For centuries, homosexuality has been considered a sin by the Christian church. Scriptures such as Genesis 19:1–11, Leviticus 18:22, and Romans 1:18–32 had always been understood to mean that any sexual thought or activity that is directed toward members of the same sex is an abomination in the sight of God. Around the same time as the sexual revolution of the 1970s, the church began to shift in its view of homosexuality. In 1968, Troy Perry founded the Metropolitan Community Church which was largely aimed at ministering to, and accepting, practising homosexuals. In 1975, the United Church of Christ (UCC) voted to end the discrimination of homosexuals. In the early 1980s, the UCC declared that homosexuality was not a matter of morality. In 1991, the same denomination exhorted its congregation to "boldly affirm, celebrate, and embrace the gifts for ministry of lesbians, gays, and bisexual persons."[8] Accompanying the UCC, the Evangelical Lutheran Church in America stated that there could be no absolute judgments drawn concerning the topic of homosexuality.[9] Presently, both the United Methodist and Episcopal denominations, while universally rejecting homosexuality, have openly allowed gay members and clergy to remain in their homosexual practices without discipline.[10]

Reinterpreting Scripture

In order for churches to accept those who practice homosexual behavior, pastors began to reinterpret those Bible passages related to homosexuality:

Genesis 19:1–11, Leviticus 18:22, Romans 1:18–32, 1 Corinthians 6:9–10, and Timothy 1:10. These passages speak either directly about the subject of homosexuality or about loving sinners.

GENESIS 19:1–11

These verses give the account of the destruction of the cities of Sodom and Gomorrah. Genesis records that the men who came to visit Lot because of his visitors said,

> Where are the men who came to you
> tonight? Bring them out to us, that we
> may know them.
>
> (v. 5, ESV)

The pro-homosexual church (PHC) states that there is no way to know for certain what the term translated "know" means. According to the PHC, this word *could* mean "to have sexual relations with," or it could mean that they were simply curious about who these men were. The PHC states that the whole account is about male–male rape.[11] The PHC further goes on to state that the overarching sin shown in this account is that of *inhospitality*.

Traditionally, this passage of Scripture has viewed

the men of Sodom as committing the sin of homosexuality. It is clear, because of Lot's reaction—which was to offer up his two daughters (v. 8)—that the men who knocked on Lot's door were looking to commit homosexual acts with the two visitors. God's response to the sin is of great importance when it comes to correctly understanding this passage. God destroyed the city filled with men who wanted to have sexual relations with the visiting men. God had not yet given the command in Scripture to stay away from homosexuality, but it was very clear that he was angered by the actions of these men. Nowhere else in history is the sin of inhospitality treated by God with sulfur and fire from heaven, whereas death was the prescribed judgment on the part of the Israelites when one of them was found to be involved in homosexual activity. It is clear, therefore, that this passage is referring to homosexuality and not lack of hospitality.

LEVITICUS 18:22

Leviticus 18 consists of a list of sexual prohibitions from God for the Israelite nation. It addresses all forms of sexual sin, including incest, bestiality, adultery, and homosexuality. Verse 22 specifically states,

> You shall not lie with a male as with a
> woman; it is an abomination.
>
> (ESV)

The PHC does not reinterpret this passage but simply places it under the category of "culturally irrelevant." It states that there were many different cultural standards that the Israelites were forced to keep, such as not eating rare steak, not eating pork, and others that are not followed today.[12] These standards were put in place in order to keep the Israelite nation separate from the Canaanite nation.

For centuries, the traditional interpretation of this passage has been literal, claiming that there are absolute morals that go beyond culture and time. Homosexuality is one of them, which is why it also shows up as a prohibition in the New Testament.[13] Traditionally, this chapter has been interpreted as an ethical chapter defining what is acceptable to God and what is not in regards to sexual acts.

ROMANS 1:18–27

Romans 1:18–27 is the apostle Paul's rendering of what happened to mankind when they ceased worshipping the Creator and started worshipping the creation. This description includes men and women committing indecent acts with members of the same sex.

The PHC interprets the punishment of God, giving them "over to degrading passions," as being caused by the people's lack of living by faith (see v. 16). In addition, the word "unnatural" (v. 26) is interpreted to signify a person who is homosexual in orientation but does not act in accordance with his or her natural desires, instead trying to fit in with society and have heterosexual relations.[14] The PHC believes that to go against that natural inclination is what is described as being "unnatural."

"Natural" refers to what is characteristic, consistent, ordinary, standard, expected, and regular. When people acted as expected and showed a certain consistency, they were acting naturally. When people did something that was surprising, beyond routine, or out of character, they were acting unnaturally. That was the sense of the word "natural" in Paul's usage.[15]

The traditional interpretation of this passage is that man started to worship the creation instead of the Creator. The ensuing punishment from God was to give them over to the passions that were flaring up within them as a result of worshipping the creation. This interpretation states not only that man ceased worshipping the Creator, but also that man inverted the proper order of male/female relations.

In his catalogue of sins in these verses, Paul lists homosexuality and lesbianism first after idolatry, not because they are the most serious sins, but because they are warning signs that a violation of reason and nature has occurred. Man has inverted God's order by worshipping the creature rather than the Creator, and, as a sign of this error, rather like the blinking red light on the dashboard of a car which is functioning improperly, God has given man up to "'dishonorable desires' in the inversion of their sexual roles."[16]

Committing homosexual acts is thus an inversion of worship, which is, in turn, punished by God by allowing an inversion of sexual preference.

1 CORINTHIANS 6:9–10 AND 1 TIMOTHY 1:10

These passages both use the term "homosexuals" and speak to those who would be caught up in those sins, as well as serving as a warning to those who might be tempted to go down the homosexual path. First Corinthians 6:9–10 speaks of the homosexual as one who will not inherit the kingdom of God, while 1 Timothy 1:10 speaks of the homosexual as disobedient and one for whom the law was created.

The PHC states that there is a wide variation in the different Bible translations of the Greek words. They claim that these words are rendered as any of the following: adulterers, homosexuals, sexual perverts, male prostitutes, sodomites, child molesters, perverts, homosexual perverts, people of infamous habits, catamites, effeminate, boy prostitutes, sissies, self-indulgent, masturbators, and practicing homosexuals.[17] The PHC claims that there is no real conclusion to which we can come, so we must take the "best available opinion of the day."[18]

The traditional interpretation of these two passages is that Paul was referring to any person who was practicing any sexual act with a person of the same gender. The Greek language is much more descriptive in nature than the English language is; thus what a modern-day English writer would simply slap a label on, the Greek writer would take time to describe. Therefore, it is the widely accepted interpretation that Paul was describing homosexual behavior in many of its various forms, not just picking out certain forms of homosexual behavior.

Implications of Each Translation

How a parent chooses to interpret the Bible is extremely significant when seeking to deal with a child who thinks he or she is a homosexual. A teen who is trying to figure out if homosexuality is a sin in the eyes of God needs to know what the Bible does indeed say about that issue. If the Bible is as ambiguous as the PHC states, the only decision that the teenager needs to make is whether or not he or she is more oriented toward the same sex or the opposite sex. The pro-homosexual interpretation will give much sympathy to, acceptance of, and encouragement for the teenager who says that he or she is attracted to people of the same sex, but who fails to deal honestly with the Scriptures.

The historical interpretation of the Scriptures, on the other hand, states that homosexuality is a sin. The Bible is clear in stating that homosexuality is an abomination in the sight of God and that those who practice this wickedness will not inherit the kingdom of heaven. The only option for the teen struggling with homosexuality is whether or not he or she is going to obey the Word of God. Obedience is shown as trust in God's Word. This can be of great comfort to the person who simply wants to have a clear-cut path on which to walk.

3

Momentum Downward: The Biblical Perspective on Homosexuality

Humans are too complicated for us to say that one thing is the root cause of a person's homosexuality. As 1 John 2:16 declares,

> For all that is in the world, the lust of
> the flesh and the lust of the eyes and
> the boastful pride of life, is not from the
> Father, but is from the world.

There are myriad factors that need to be brought into the light and sorted out if you as a parent are going to help your teenager get out of the bondage of habitual sin. Homosexual thoughts and desires are no different.

For clarity's sake, there needs to be a distinction made between *primary causes* and *secondary influences*. Primary causes are those that directly cause homosexual tendencies. Secondary influences are those circumstances that influence and exacerbate the temptation toward homosexual behavior. Primary causes may be likened to a match that starts a fire, while secondary influences may be compared to the wind, amount of oxygen, and fuel source that decide how fast and hot the fire burns. It doesn't matter how much wind, oxygen, and fuel one has; if there is no flame, there will be no fire. Likewise, if the primary causes for homosexuality are not present, the secondary influences will not bring about homosexuality in the teenager.

There are two primary causes: the heart, and the exchange of worship.

The Heart

When children are little and the question "Why?" is asked of them about something they have done, they rarely give an accurate account of their actions. This does not change as the child gets older; thus most teenagers, when asked "Why?" give an answer similar to that of a toddler. Their answers usually consist of "I don't know" or "I just felt like it." Scripture is very different and thus can aid you if you are trying to help your struggling teenager. Mark 7:20–23 states,

> And he said, "What comes out of a

person is what defiles him. For from within, out of the heart of man, come evil thoughts, sexual immorality, theft, murder, adultery, coveting, wickedness, deceit, sensuality, envy, slander, pride, foolishness. All these evil things come from within, and they defile a person."

(ESV)

Jesus is very clear in stating that the heart is the source of everything that is said and done. There are no accidental decisions, no slips of the tongue; no action taken is unintentional. The motivation for everything that we do originates in the heart. This is true of teens who struggle with both homosexual thoughts and actions. The struggling teen needs to be taught that his or her heart is the originator of everything that he or she thinks, feels, says, and does. There is nothing that can motivate the teen to commit homosexual acts unless his or her heart first gives approval for those influences to impact his or her thinking.

A DESCRIPTION OF THE HUMAN HEART

John Calvin described the human heart as an idol factory pumping out idol after idol. This simply means that the human heart is so sinful that it will take anything good, bad, or indifferent and start to serve it rather than the One who created it. Jeremiah 17:9 gives perhaps the best description of the human heart:

> The heart is more deceitful than all else,
> And is desperately sick;
> Who can understand it?

There are three descriptive words that need to be unpacked before the teenager can have as full a comprehension as possible of the condition under which he or she lives.

First, our hearts are "deceitful" above "all else." "All else" means "everything," an all-inclusive term that means that there is not a single thing that is more deceptive in the world than that which resides within each of us. The implication is that the person in whom this deceptive heart resides is not capable of knowing exactly what his or her motivations are, nor of why he or she is doing a particular thing. The deceptive nature of that heart will conceal the real motivations for thoughts and actions. For the struggling teen, this means that there is no chance that he or she can know the reason for the choice to sinfully think about homosexuality, nor for the choice to commit acts of homosexuality.

Second, this verse describes the human heart as "desperately sick," or "incurably sick." There is absolutely nothing that any human being can do to cure this condition. Much like a person who is diagnosed with congestive heart failure can only be saved by a heart transplant, so the teenager who is dealing with homosexual thoughts and desires can only hope to be saved by receiving a cure that will take care of the heart problem, not just the symptom of homosexuality.[19]

The third and final description that is not explicitly given but implied is that our hearts are *unknowable* by any other human. This places the final stamp of hopelessness on the condition of the human heart. The human heart is not only unknowable by the person in which it resides, it is also unknowable by any other person who might try to understand it. The logic of this is quite profound. If all human hearts are the same, and no single human can understand his or her own heart, it follows that no human can know or understand the heart of any other human either. This places all man-centered therapy and psychology under the category of "ignorance" when it comes to helping the struggling teenager. If Scripture is correct and the motivations of the human heart are unknowable to anyone else, all human attempts will only fail.

Jesus went to great lengths to make sure that his disciples understood just what it is that defiles a person and where the motivations for doing anything come from (Mark 7:14–23). All sin, including homosexuality, is a matter of the heart. The teenager's heart is deceitful and will keep him or her from knowing why he or she is motivated toward homosexuality and not toward other sins. The heart is incurable, which means that the teen's motivations will continuously be evil until a new heart is given. In addition, there is no other human who can aid the teen to understand why he or she is sinning in this way. The picture that God's Word presents is of a situation that is hopeless aside from God's help.

THE ORIGIN OF THE SINFUL HEART

So where does this heart come from? Is a person born with this heart, or does he or she develop it over a period of time? King David states in Psalm 51:5 that he was born sinful and was even conceived as sinful. Romans 5:12 states that, because sin was brought into the world through Adam, that same sin spread to all men and women. Ephesians 2:3 says that, by nature, humans are "children of wrath." These three passages of Scripture, along with many others, portray the human heart as sinful from the very moment of conception.

It is very important for your teen and for you as parents to know this, because it means that this condition is not due to some outside force that victimized your teenager in some way. It is because of the passing down of a sinful nature from Adam that your teenager has a tendency to sin in the area of homosexuality.

It is also important for your teenager to know that, if he or she did not struggle with homosexuality, there would be a struggle with some other expression of sin. Your teenager is a sinner at the core, which is why he or she sins; it is not the other way around. In his book *A Biblical Guide to Counseling the Sexual Addict*, Steve Gallagher appropriately states the following:

> *There's not a person alive who doesn't have to overcome some inherent attraction to sin. The fact that some individuals have a propensity toward homosexual lust shouldn't surprise us. Homosexual lust is a result—either directly or indirectly—of the fall [sinful heart].*[20]

This means that the struggling teen could have lived in a perfect world, as far as circumstances are concerned, and the human heart would still have been motivating him or her to sin in the area of homosexuality or in other ways.

APPLICATION OF THIS TRUTH

Breaking through the victimizing theories this world offers and bringing to your teenager the truth that he or she is not alone in this world, struggling against sin, will be a relief. It is at this point that verses such as 1 Corinthians 10:13 should be ministered:

> No temptation has overtaken you but such as is common to man; and God is faithful, who will not allow you to be tempted beyond what you are able, but with the temptation will provide the way of escape also, so that you will be able to endure it.

The teenager should understand that homo-sexuality, much like any other sin, is the sinful heart's way of revealing that God is not the One who is worshipped there.

SOLUTION FOR THE HEART PROBLEM

The most important application for the homosexual comes in the form of knowing how to fix the problem. If the problem is a sinful heart that is wicked, desperately sick, and unknowable, the only answer is to have a new heart placed within by Someone who knows exactly what kind of heart is needed, how to get such a new heart, and how to put that new heart in place. This new heart will give your teenager a godly perspective which will allow him or her to clearly see the way out of the sinful temptations in life. Hence the gospel should be clearly presented to your struggling teenager at this time.

This gospel presentation is a call for the teen to repent of his or her sin and to place his or her faith in Jesus Christ as the only hope for salvation. From a practical standpoint, this involves two distinct acts. First and foremost, there needs to be a repentance from sin. Jesus says in Mark 1:15,

> The time is fulfilled, and the kingdom
> of God is at hand; repent and believe in
> the gospel.

This repentance is nothing less than admitting that we are sinners who deserve the wrath of God for what we have done. If your teenager is unwilling to admit this, there is no hope of true change.

Additionally there needs to be a believing and trusting in Jesus Christ's life, death, and resurrection:

> If you confess with your mouth Jesus
> as Lord, and believe in your heart that
> God raised Him from the dead, you will
> be saved; for with the heart a person
> believes, resulting in righteousness, and
> with the mouth he confesses, resulting
> in salvation.
>
> (Romans 10:9–10)

Christ lived his entire life perfectly because he knew that we, your struggling teenager included, would be unable to live a perfect life. Christ faced every temptation, every demand, every struggle, just as your teen is doing—yet Christ did not sin. The struggling teen needs to have the perfection of Christ credited to him or her in order to be treated by God just as God treats his own Son, Jesus Christ. Placing personal faith *in the life of Christ* effectively moves the teenager from the identity of a homosexual to the identity of a child of God.

Additionally, the teenager also needs to place his or her faith *in the death of Christ*. The death of Christ satisfied the wrath of God—the very wrath that was stored up for the teenager due to his or her sin. There is such hope in knowing that God is no longer accumulating wrath, but will instead pour out more and more of his love.

Finally, the teenager needs to place his or her faith *in the resurrection of Christ*. The apostle Paul said that "we are of all men most to be pitied" if Jesus Christ did not rise from the dead (1 Corinthians 15:19). Christ's resurrection proved who he was, thus conquering sin and the death that comes with that sin. Hope beyond hope is given to the teen who is truly broken over sin upon the realization that, because of Christ's life, death, and resurrection, God now welcomes him or her with open arms as his own child upon whom he can pour blessings.

This gospel hope is the only answer to the problem of teenagers and homosexuality. Without this kind of hope that comes through a genuine heart change, there will be no lasting godly change, and most likely your teen will return to the lifestyle of homosexuality.

The Exchange of Worship

The other primary cause of the teen struggling with homosexual desires is related to the purpose for which we were all created. Glorifying God by worshipping him and enjoying him forever is the intended purpose of every single person.[21] Adam and Eve were created by God in order to commune with him, obey him, love him, and honor him. The angels were created by God to serve and worship him. Throughout Scripture, we are told of the glory of God and how we are to worship God because of that glory:

» "I will give thanks to You, O Lord my God, with all my heart, and will glorify Your name forever" (Psalm 86:12).

» "Hear the word of the LORD, you who tremble at His Word: 'Your brothers who hate you, who exclude you for My name's sake, have said, "Let the LORD be glorified, that we may see your joy." But they will be put to shame'" (Isaiah 66:5).

» "For you have been bought with a price: therefore glorify God in your body" (1 Corinthians 6:20).

» "Whether, then, you eat or drink or whatever you do, do all to the glory of God" (1 Corinthians 10:31).

Every human being was created for worship. When the worship that naturally flows out of the heart is not directed at God, it becomes unnatural worship, and it is followed by unnatural actions. This is true for any sin that any person gets involved with. When feeling good (emotions are part of creation) is worshipped above the One who created the emotion, the unnatural twisting of the human heart makes a person seek those things that will make him or her feel good at the cost of all else. This is why an alcoholic[22] will forsake God, family, a job, driving privileges, and so much more in order to keep drinking alcohol. Likewise, the teen who is struggling with homosexuality will do what seems unnatural to the obedient Christian, by dwelling on thoughts about those of the same sex. If left to continue, these unnatural thoughts will usually lead the teen to forsake family members and friends, and finally God.

STEP 1: EXCHANGING GOD FOR AN IMAGE

Romans 1:18–32 gives a graphic description of what the exchange of worship looks like. The apostle

Paul recounts the exchange of the worship of the Creator (God) for the worship of the creation (man; see Romans 1:24–25, ESV). This process of exchanging what is natural for what is unnatural started with not honoring God or giving him thanks. This honoring and giving thanks is, in effect, worship.

A key component to understanding this Scripture is to understand that those who stopped worshipping God did not stop worshipping, as this would have been impossible. As is recorded in verse 23, they exchanged the glory of the immortal God for images made to look like mortal man, birds, animals and reptiles. This was an exchange of God's glory for the glory of a manmade image. It was this unnatural twisting of the One who should have been glorified that brought about unnatural actions.

Step 2: An Exchanged Reality
The result of this lack of honoring and thanking God was futile thinking and a darkened heart. It is this futility and darkness of heart that allowed people to think they were wise when in fact they were fools. This exchanging of worship led to an exchange of everything else in their lives. Where there was once light, there was now darkness;

where there was once humility, there was now vanity; and where there was once wisdom, there was now foolishness. Verse 21 points directly back to the purpose for which humanity was created. When God is served, God defines reality, purpose, value, and everything else that humans seem to crave. He decides what is foolish and what is wise. When man, or what he has created, is worshipped, it is that creation that defines man's reality, purpose, value, and so on.

STEP 3: AN EXCHANGE IN FUNCTION

It is at this point that God allowed people to be taken over by the lusts of their own hearts. The unnatural lust for the same sex is not handed down from God, as this would be going against God's nature. *The seeking of the same sex is a natural consequence of an unnatural worship-exchange.* God simply allows that which is already in the heart to come to fruition in order to give the world a physical manifestation of what has happened in the heart. It was only by God's patient restraining hand that any of those people mentioned in Romans 1 did not immediately seek out their own lusts. As previously stated, man is born in a sinful state; thus he has all that he needs within his heart to bring forth sins such as homosexuality.

Once God saw fit to hand people over to their own lusts, it took no time at all for them to exchange that which was natural (heterosexuality) for that which was unnatural (homosexuality).

In respect to the struggling teen who has not yet given in to temptation, it is only by God's restraining hand that he or she has not fallen into the sin of homosexuality. The teen needs to understand that, if he or she continues to worship the creation, God will eventually lift his restraining hand from that teen's life. Once that happens, the pull into an active homosexual life will be yielded to quickly and with little effort. This strong warning needs to be given to the teen by you, as parents, and by others who love him or her.

Step 4: All Sin Is Deemed Good

Exchanging the worship of God leads to a whole new perception of life. This allows people to see homosexuality not only as decent and good, but also as the way things should be. At this point, the dam has broken, so to speak. Everything that was once condemned is re-examined and redefined as good. Paul states,

> And just as they did not see fit to
> acknowledge God any longer, God

> gave them over to a depraved mind, to
> do those things which are not proper,
> being filled with all unrighteousness,
> wickedness, greed, evil; full of envy,
> murder, strife, deceit, malice; they
> are gossips, slanderers, haters of God,
> insolent, arrogant, boastful, inventors
> of evil, disobedient to parents, without
> understanding, untrustworthy,
> unloving, unmerciful ...
>
> (Romans 1:28–31)

Reality has turned a complete 180 degrees. What starts out as an exchange of worship leads to a complete life change that people cannot reverse in and of themselves. It is only God's restraining hand that holds back the sinful waters that seek to destroy them. Now that God has released those waters, those individuals are at the mercy of the sin that has consumed them.

STEP 5: FULFILLING THE EXCHANGE

One final aspect is found in Romans 1:32:

> Although they know the ordinance of
> God, that those who practice such things
> are worthy of death, they not only do the

> same, *but also give hearty approval to*
> *those who practice them.*

This final act of giving hearty approval to others who follow their actions seals what they have sought to do all along. They started off by exchanging the worship of God for the worship of something created. Self-rule has been the goal all along. This goal was what Adam and Eve sought in the Garden of Eden, and, from that point on, all humanity has sought the same thing. They have decided not only what they will worship, but also to tell other people what they should worship. The end result is a god-complex in which people see themselves as God and want others to view them as God.

APPLICATION OF THIS TRUTH

An understanding of these verses can provide the struggling teen with great hope. The biggest area of hope lies in the fact that he or she has not been given a life-sentence to live as a homosexual. The truth found in these verses can provide step-by-step instructions away from the thoughts that are probably dominating the teen's thought-life. The cause of homosexuality is the person's exchange of the glory of God for the glory of the image of man and a lack of thankfulness to God. If this exchange of worship was what caused this unnatural twisting and exchange of worship, twisting it back toward the One who naturally should be worshipped, glorified, and thanked will set your teen back on the proper path of obedience and set him or her free from the power of homosexual temptations. There are, of course, extenuating circumstances that the teen will need to have some help with, such as friends, coworkers, forms of entertainment, and so forth. A truly repentant teen will be willing to let go of those things and cling to the hope that is found in Christ.

The sinful condition of the human heart and the exchange of worship are the two primary causes that Scripture gives for the outworking of homosexuality, thoughts and desires included, in the life of a teenager. These two causes are not given an age limit, cultural limitations, situational limitations, or any other constraints. "All have sinned and fall short of the glory of God" (Romans 3:23), which means that all people have the potential to fall into the sin of homosexuality.

The only hope for the one struggling with homosexuality is to repent of personal sin and believe in the life, death, and resurrection of

Jesus Christ. Jesus Christ lived a perfect life because we could not. He died a horrific death so that we would not have to spend an eternity experiencing the awful wrath of God for the sins that we commit throughout our lives. Christ rose triumphantly in order to defeat sin and free us to live for him for eternity. There is no hope outside of this magnificent, glorious good news. However, for those who have repented and placed their faith in Christ, they have been washed, cleansed, and set apart by God as his children for eternity.

4

How to Help Your Teen

Before seeking to help someone else get out of sin, it is always right and proper for any Christian to personally examine his or her own life for sin. This principle is found in Matthew 7:1–5, where Jesus says that we should take the log out of our own eyes before we take the speck out of someone else's eye. You, as a Christian parent of a teen struggling with homosexual behavior, are no different. Parents who truly want to help their teenagers out of homosexuality should examine themselves first in order to see if there are any glaring sins that they have openly been involved in, so as not to be hypocritical when coming to help their children. Some things to think about are shows that you habitually watch on TV, music that you listen to on a regular basis, how much time you spend with God in prayer and Bible study, how frequently your family attends church, how often your family has devotions together, how much you are focused on outward appearance (the gym, tanning salon, clothing, etc.), and how obedient you have been as a biblical husband, wife, mother, or father.

Self-Examination

If you do find glaring areas of sin in your life, it is right and proper to remember that you did not cause your teen to sin in the area of homosexuality. Before you go and confront your teen, be an example and follow the repentance process by thinking about what you have done, confessing what you have done to God and to your teen, and then letting the teen know of the changes you are putting into place. This brings God honor and glory, and shows your teenager that you are willing to do what you are about to ask him or her to do.

Repentance

When it comes time to confront your teen about the sinful actions of homosexuality, it is key to look for heart change that comes about only as a result of repentance. We humans have a myriad of motivations for changing behavior, but most are not concerned with changing into Christlikeness. Repentance is change at the heart level, which is the only change that will last for a lifetime. The repentance process starts with thinking long and hard about the sins that have been committed. It is not merely feeling bad for what we have done; rather it is truly thinking about how we have sinned against God and other people. For the teen, this thinking should involve a significant amount of time in God's Word, getting God's viewpoint on what he or she has done.

Confession

This should lead to a proper confession to both God and those sinned against. This confession should include words similar to "I was wrong for [specific sin]; will you please forgive me?" At the very least, there should be an admission of guilt and a request for forgiveness. If those two items are not included in the confession, then, out of grace and mercy, you should patiently ask your teen questions that will reveal if he or she is really repentant and wants to change. Some examples of these types of question are:

» "We know that you feel horrible for what you have done. Would you like us to forgive you for what you have done?"

» "We can see that you are sorry about this. Do you want to change and go in a new direction?"

Change of Life

This confession should then lead to a drastic change in the teen's life. There should be a complete 180-degree change in most areas of his or her life. Ephesians 4:22–24 gives the biblical process of change that the teen needs to go through. This equation is seen through the commands "lay aside the old self," "be renewed in the spirit of your mind," and "put on the new self." The areas of life that should show signs of a biblical heart change might include choice of music, movies, job, TV shows, friends, appearance, vocabulary, social-network associations, clothing, where and how he or she spends time, as well as how your teen starts to talk about God and all matters related to God. If there is not a drastic change in most of these areas, there is a good chance that the teen will fall back into homosexual temptation.

CONCLUSION: HOPE BEYOND HOPE

First and foremost, you need to remember that you did not cause your teen to partake in homosexual behavior. If you find yourself feeling as if you have caused your teen to fall prey to this sin, spend some time thinking through these words:

> Then the word of the LORD came to me, saying, "What do you mean by using this proverb concerning the land of Israel saying, 'The fathers eat the sour grapes, but the children's teeth are set on edge?' As I live," declares the LORD, "you are surely not going to use this proverb in Israel anymore. Behold, all souls are Mine; the soul of the father as well as the soul of the son is Mine. The soul who sins will die."
>
> (Ezekiel 18:1–4)

In this verse, God forbids the use of a proverb that people were using to excuse their sin. At the end of God's rebuke, God says that the soul that sins is the soul that will die. He is saying that we are responsible for our own sins. No one can make us do what we do. Parent, there is nothing that you did to cause your teen to choose to act this way. Remember that this sin comes from an exchange of worship, not from sinful parents.

Additionally, this sin is not permanent. Many people have stopped practicing homosexual acts and have gone on to bring honor and glory to God with their lives. In 1 Corinthians 6:11 God states,

> Such *were* some of you; but you *were*
> washed, but you *were* sanctified, but you
> *were* justified in the name of the Lord
> Jesus Christ and in the Spirit of our God.
> (Emphasis mine)

This verse comes at the end of a long list of people who at one time were not going to inherit the kingdom of heaven, but, due to the work of Christ, they were now going to spend eternity with him. Within that list are those who had committed acts of homosexuality.

It is good to keep a long-term gospel perspective

as you walk beside your teen through the process of repentance. In order to do this, you will need to remind both yourself and your teen of the gospel every day. The gospel is simply the life, death, and resurrection of Jesus Christ. Christ lived the life that we could not live. He bore the wrath of God in his death so that we would not have to. And he rose again from the dead so that we might have life. If you don't remember this daily, you and your teen will forget it and start to go back to a works-based way of living. This happens when people are only concerned with the behavior and not the heart. If you do this, you will get tired of the walk and quit. Your teen faces this same struggle. If he or she does not remember the gospel often, the road away from homosexuality will be too hard, and he or she will simply fall back into the sin.

Depending upon how deeply your teen has gone into the sin of homosexuality, the path of repentance could be filled with many points of struggle and repeated sin. The gospel is the hope to hang on to during those moments of failure. The process of becoming more and more like Christ is not one of perfection but of responding to each moment as Christ commands. There will be times when your teen faces temptation and he or she will decide to be obedient because of the work that Christ has done. Rejoice, and make much of those times with your teen. There will also be those times when your teen will face temptation and fail. You will then need to remind him or her of the gospel and Christ's work on his or her behalf so that your teen does not get discouraged and give up. In those moments, remind your teen to go through the repentance process of thinking about the sin he or she has committed, confessing that sin, and changing the way that he or she lives life.

Personal Application Projects

For Parents

1. REMEMBER THE TRUTH
When dealing with any rebellious teenager, it is
always good to remember where the rebellion
originates: in the heart of the one who rebels.
Read the following verses and write down
in your own words what God says about the
one who is in sin and where the sin begins:
Ezekiel 18:1–4; Romans 6:23; Jeremiah 17:9;
Mark 7:14–23; Matthew 13:15; and Ecclesiastes 9:3.
Now read this next set of verses and record in
your own words what Scripture says about God's
sovereign control over every situation, good
and bad: Romans 8:28–29; 1 Corinthians 10:13;
Isaiah 55:8–9; 2 Timothy 1:9; Ephesians 2:8–9;
and Philippians 4:4–7. When you are done, spend
some time in prayer, thanking God for revealing
to you the condition of your son's or daughter's
heart, as well as for remaining in control of every
single circumstance in this situation.

2. REMOVE THE LOG

While parents never cause their children to sin, they can influence their children and exasperate them, thus provoking them and moving them toward sin. Read the following verses and record in your own words what they teach about how you personally should prepare for a confrontation with your son or daughter: Matthew 7:1–5; Philippians 2:3–4; and James 4:1–3. Spend some time in prayer and meditation, asking the Lord to reveal to you any ways in which you have sinned against your teenager. This could take two or three hours. After you have done this, plan for some uninterrupted time with your teen, seeking his or her forgiveness for your own sins that God has revealed to you.

3. RESTORE THE RELATIONSHIP

As with any relationship that has been damaged by sin, it is important to seek restoration. Full restoration can only come about with full repentance on the part of your teen. However, you can make it easier for your son or daughter to ask for forgiveness and seek repentance. Pull out your calendar and mark out thirty minutes to an hour each day of the week that you will set aside for nurturing your relationship with your teen. Fulfill these appointments for a full month. Additionally, plan two extended "dates," each of four hours or more, with the purpose of two-way communication with your son or daughter. Stay away from movies, sporting events, and other activities that do not encourage communication but usually result in passive observation. Be sure to communicate to your son or daughter what changes you are going to implement and carry through on yourself for the sake of your relationship.

For Your Teen

These projects are designed to help the teen struggling with homosexuality to recognize what he or she did that was sinful, and how it has offended God and hurt family members or close friends.

1. CONTEMPLATION LOG

Read the following verses and write down the meaning of each in your own words: Genesis 19:1–29; 39:1–12; Leviticus 18:22; 20:13; Psalm 119:9–11; Proverbs 7:1–27; 13:20; 17:14; 18:10; 19:3; 22:3; 26:20–22; 29:18; Matthew 5:27–32; Acts 20:32; Romans 1:24–32; Romans 6:1–23; 8:32, 37; 12:1–2;

13:11–14; Ephesians 4:7–16; 1 Corinthians 6:9–11;
10:13; 1 Corinthians 9:24–27; Galatians 5:24;
1 Timothy 1:8–11; Jude 7–8. Now take some time
to write out in your own words the sins that you
have committed and how they have impacted your
family. If you find this hard to imagine or think of,
interview your dad, mom, and siblings to find out
just how your actions have hurt them.

2. *Confession Log*
This assignment should help you keep track of
what you have asked forgiveness for, as well as
when forgiveness has been granted. After you have
taken time to contemplate, schedule time with
each of your family members in order to ask them
for forgiveness for your sin against them. The
contemplation log is a great item to use during
this time so that you don't forget anything while
you are talking with them. Make sure you say, "I
was wrong for _____; will you forgive me?"
Make sure to give them enough time to think
about what you have said. It is OK if they need
some time to think about your request. Continue
to remind them that you are changing and want
things to be corrected. After you have asked for
forgiveness and have been forgiven, record the
date, time, what was forgiven, and who forgave.

This log will help you remember what you have taken care of biblically, as well as what you have not. Additionally, should you at a later time feel guilty for what you have done, you can go back and remind yourself that you are no longer guilty because you have been forgiven.

3. AREAS OF LIFE CHANGE

Read Ephesians 4:1–32. Examine all areas of your life to see what has been affected by the sin of homosexuality. These areas include sex, social life, family, church, work, school, free time, abilities, sleep, and nutrition. The idea here is not to find a cause for your homosexual behavior but to examine those areas to see if your homosexual behavior has influenced them. Once these areas have been examined, the goal is to put off those areas that have been affected by the sin and to put on new ways of living. For instance, you may stay up late at night texting, in order to keep your sin a secret. Examining your sleep habits will reveal that homosexual behavior has invaded them. If you are interested in forsaking the sin, you may therefore need to forsake your phone as well as staying up late. The enforcement of a strict bedtime should result after examining this area of life.

4. GOSPEL PRESENTATION/REMINDER

In order to help remind yourself of the gospel, write the following sentence on ten separate 3x5 cards: "My hope is found in the life, death, and resurrection of Christ alone." Place those cards in ten very obvious places so that you will be reminded of the gospel frequently throughout the day. You could place them on your computer screen, inside your school locker, on the back of your cell phone, inside your wallet, on the keyboard of your laptop, by the bathroom mirror, and on your alarm clock, refrigerator door, pantry door, and bedroom door.

Where Can I Get More Help?

The following organizations and Web sites can be of assistance for both teenagers struggling with homosexuality and parents who want to help.

Setting Captives Free: www.settingcaptivesfree.com

Christian Counseling and Education Foundation: www.ccef.org

Exodus International: www.exodusinternational.org

Harvest USA: www.harvestusa.org

Pure Life Ministries: www.purelifeministries.org

The National Association of Nouthetic Counselors: www.nanc.org

END NOTES

1 In addition to an attempt to explain away homosexual behavior by biology, there has been a concerted effort by psychologists to make homosexuality appear to be normal behavior. A look through the Diagnostic and Statistical Manual of Mental Disorders (DSM) from 1973 onwards will reveal the progression of homosexuality from abnormal deviant behavior to something that is no longer mentioned.

2 Alfred Kinsey, Sexual Behavior in the Human Male (Philadelphia: Saunders Press, 1948), 625.

3 Simon LeVay, "A Difference in Hypothalamic Structure between Heterosexual and Homosexual Men," in Science, 253, 1034–1037.

4 Simon LeVay, "Sex and the Brain," in Discover, 15/3 (March 1994), 64.

5 Michael J. Bailey and D. S. Benishay, "Familial Aggregation of Female Sexual Orientation," in American Journal of Psychiatry, 150, 272–277.

6 Randolph E. Schmid, "Differing Brain Response Found in Homosexual, Heterosexual Men," Associated Press, May 10, 2005; available at: othersiderainbow.blogspot.com/.

7 Michael S. Piazza, Holy Homosexuals (Dallas: Sources of Hope, 1997), 1–3.

8 Joseph P. Gudel, "'That Which is Unnatural':

Homosexuality in Society, the Church, and Scripture," in Christian Research Institute Journal in Internet Christian Library: iclnet.org/pub/resources/text/cri/cri-jrnl/web/crj0108a.html.

9 Evangelical Lutheran Church in America, Human Sexuality and the Christian Faith (Minneapolis: ELCA, 1991), 44.

10 Gudel, That Which is Unnatural, 3.

11 Daniel A. Helminiak, What the Bible Really Says about Homosexuality (New Mexico: Alamo Square Press, 2000), 45.

12 Gudel, That Which is Unnatural, 5.

13 Ibid.

14 Piazza, Holy Homosexuals, 43.

15 Helminiak, What the Bible Really Says, 79.

16 Richard F. Lovelace, Homosexuality and the Church (Old Tappan, NJ: Fleming H. Revell, 1978), 71.

17 Helminiak, What the Bible Really Says, 106.

18 Ibid. 107.

19 Many times the symptom of the sinful condition is dealt with (homosexuality), without seeking to cure the root cause of the symptom. It is important to keep the symptom separate from the cause.

20 Steve Gallagher, A Biblical Guide to Counseling the Sexual Addict (Dry Ridge, KY: Pure Life Ministries, 2004), 107.

21 The Shorter Catechism, Question 1.

22 This term is used not to denote a disease, rather to state in today's terms what the Bible labels a "drunkard."

BOOKS IN THE HELP! SERIES INCLUDE...

(More titles in preparation)